DELTICS
THE LAST YEAR

DELTICS
THE LAST YEAR

ALASTAIR McLEAN

TEMPUS

To the memory of my loving mother, Margaret B. McLean
(1926–2006)

Frontispiece: 55008 approaching Calton Tunnel, Edinburgh with 1S08
0705 Newcastle-Edinburgh on 2 May 1981. This train was often a
Deltic-hauled and they mastered this service with ease. They were due
into Edinburgh at 0923 but in this photograph the 0915 train to Kings
Cross can be seen leaving in the background. 55008 had an easy day in
Edinburgh just shunting some ECS at Waverley, from the Birmingham
train. The loco then returned to Haymarket for a rest. It would more
than likely have headed south that night on a sleeper train.

First published 2005, reprinted 2007

Tempus Publishing Limited
Cirencester Road, Chalford,
Stroud, Gloucestershire, GL6 8PE
www.tempus-publishing.com

© Alastair McLean, 2005

The right of Alastair McLean to be identified as the Author
of this work has been asserted in accordance with the
Copyrights, Designs and Patents Act 1988.

British Library Cataloguing in Publication Data.
A catalogue record for this book is available from the British Library.

ISBN 978 0 7524 3559 6

Typesetting and origination by Tempus Publishing Limited.
Printed in Great Britain.

Contents

Foreword

British Railways was in a major programme of modernisation and converting from steam to diesel traction in the 1950s and early 1960s. Plans were well in place for looking at replacing steam with diesel traction on the East Coast Main Line. A prototype Deltic had completed a successful trial period on the route and an order was placed for twenty-two production units. The builder was the English Electric Co. Ltd and the new locomotives were to be built at their Vulcan Foundry at Newton-Le-Willows. The locomotives would operate the prestigious East Coast Main Line (ECML) from London to Edinburgh, the spine of British Railways. The Deltic locomotive was designed around two Napier Deltic D18/25 engines providing a massive 3,300 horsepower. This was by far the most powerful diesel locomotive in the British Railways fleet. They had a top speed of 100mph but were timed on many occasions at speeds of up to 120mph and even 125mph.

The production Deltics were delivered to traffic during 1961 with the final unit, D9021, entering service on 2 May 1962. With very short lay-over times between duties, the introduction of the Deltics meant that only a small fleet of locomotives were needed for the ECML, utilising the class to the full.

The locomotives were named after racehorses and British army regiments. The racehorses were allocated to Finsbury Park MPD in London and the Scottish regiments were allocated to Haymarket MPD, Edinburgh, while the English regiments were based at Gateshead MPD, Newcastle. These depots were responsible for their maintenance and Doncaster Works was where major servicing and overhaul of the fleet was carried out. The ECML was transformed by the Deltics, bringing speed and punctuality to the express service.

In 1978, with the introduction of the 125mph High Speed Trains (HST), the Deltics were moved to semi-fast, cross-country duties and a mixed selection of trains. Haymarket and Gateshead lost their allocation of Deltics with their fleets moving to York MPD. The Deltics still operated with distinction on their new charges, with the 'Hull Executive' train at the time being the fasted locomotive hauled train in Britain. *Meld* worked the inaugural train and was denied a planned finale of working the final down 'Hull Executive' on 2 January 1981, due to her early withdrawal.

The Deltics also spread their operational area at this time. It was not uncommon to see them at Aberdeen, Liverpool, Hull, Manchester and Carstairs. Even Glasgow had an occasional Deltic appearance. More rail enthusiasts were following the locomotives, too. They were receiving unprecidented interest not seen in any diesel locomotive, in fact not seen since steam traction was withdrawn from Britain's railways. Every station on the ECML had crowds of enthusiasts watching every move the locomotives made.

The Deltics were so popular that four were nominated to work railtours in the final year of operation. These were 55002, 55009, 55015 and 55022. 55002 was already in her original two-tone green, a project paid for by the National Railway Museum. These four Deltics were serviced at York and even 55009 was repainted. The four special Deltics looked marvellous.

Most of the railtours were operated by one of these Deltics, but on occasion another Deltic was used. The most unusual railtour was 55021, operated from Edinburgh to Oban on two different days. I will cover this railtour later in the book.

The Deltics were gradually being withdrawn. By the beginning of November 1981, there were only thirteen locomotives remaining in the fleet. Just after mid-November the last Deltic came out of Doncaster Works after a repair, the locomotive involved being 55017.

Even at this late time in their lives the Deltics were still substituted for failed HSTs on all or part of the ECML. 55017 had a strange duty in December 1981. The locomotive operated a set of Mk3 sleeper coaches from Edinburgh to Aberdeen. This trial was unusual because Deltics were officially not allowed to operate the new coaches. Was British Rail planning to put the Deltics on the new sleepers? A question we will never know the answer to.

The Prototype Deltic at the Science Museam London

The finale was drawing near and it was to be a railtour from London to Edinburgh and return. Which Deltic would be involved? It was decided to use 55015 northbound and 55022 southbound. Most of the Deltics were withdrawn officially on 31 December except 55002, 55009, 55015 and 55022. Back-up locomotives were needed in case there were problems with the two allocated Deltics. 55015 operated the 'Deltic Scotsman Farewell' from Kings Cross to Edinburgh and 55022 operated the train southbound. Thousands turned out to witness the railtour; history was being made. Not since steam locomotives were withdrawn was there such a great interest in a locomotive class. Even national television recorded the event.

Number	Original British Railways Number	Name	Withdrawal Date
55001	D9001	St Paddy	5 January 1980
55002	D9002	The King's Own Yorkshire Light Infantry	2 January 1982
55003	D9003	Meld	31 December 1980
55004	D9004	Queens Own Highlander	1 November 1981
55005	D9005	The Prince of Wales's Own Regiment of Yorkshire	8 February 1981
55006	D9006	The Fife & Forfar Yeomanry	8 February 1981
55007	D9007	Pinza	31 December 1981
55008	D9008	The Green Howards	31 December 1981
55009	D9009	Alycidon	2 January 1982
55010	D9010	The King's Own Scottish Borderer	24 December 1981
55011	D9011	The Royal Northumberland Fusiliers	8 November 1981
55012	D9012	Crepello	31 May 1981
55013	D9013	The Black Watch	20 December 1981
55014	D9014	The Duke of Wellington's Regiment	22 November 1981
55015	D9015	Tulyar	2 January 1982
55016	D9016	Gordon Highlander	30 December 1981
55017	D9017	The Durham Light Infantry	31 December 1981
55018	D9018	Ballymoss	10 October 1981
55019	D9019	Royal Highland Fusilier	31 December 1981
55020	D9020	Nimbus	5 January 1980
55021	D9021	Argyll & Sutherland Highlander	31 December 1981
55022	D9000	Royal Scots Grey	2 January 1982

I was introduced to the Deltics in 1971 when I travelled a circular tour with a school friend and his father. We travelled to Edinburgh by train, then to Newcastle behind a Deltic. What a great run this was! I had never seen or heard a locomotive like this before. We changed trains at Newcastle for Leeds, where I heard the familar sound of another Deltic. Due to time constraints we could not go 'close quarters' to see this magnificent locomotive. Through various works and depot 'open days' a Deltic was provided as an exhibit during the early 1970s. Living in the west of Scotland, a Deltic was a rare sight. I had changed from a rail enthusiast to a Deltic enthusiast.

I witnessed the demise of such a great class of locomotives in the final years. Sad times but great camaraderie among the enthusiasts, at this time. This book is dedicated to all the enthusiasts during the swan song of the Deltics.

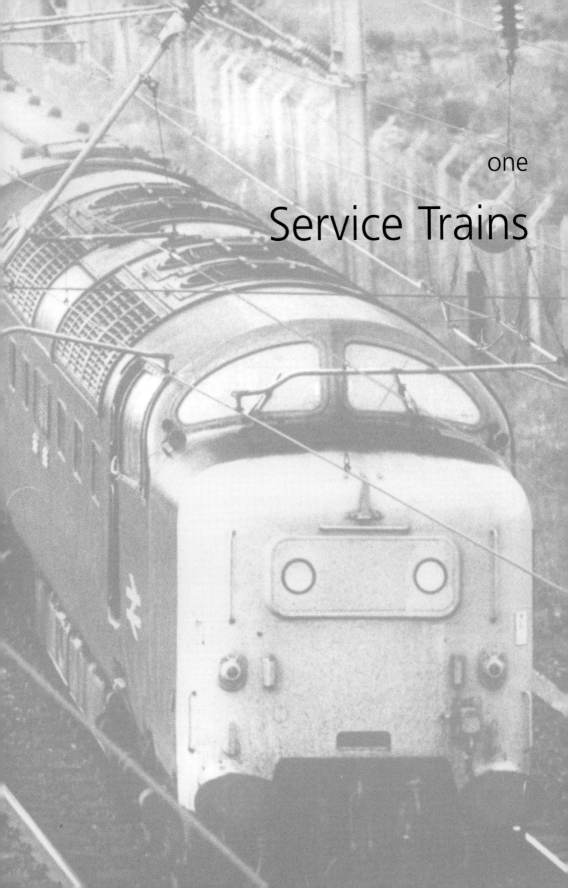

one

Service Trains

55022 has just arrived at Edinburgh Waverley with the 0550 London Kings Cross-Aberdeen train (1S12). This was a popular Deltic duty with the locomotive normally being replaced at Edinburgh, as in this case. Sometimes a Deltic was changed for another Deltic. The date here is 27 September 1980.

55015 is in the foreground and 55002 is in the background at Edinburgh Waverly. *Tulyar* had earlier worked the 0705 (1S08) Newcastle to Edinburgh service. 55002 is preparing to work the 0950 Edinburgh-Plymouth train. The clock above the old North British Hotel is showing 0950, but it was traditionally set five minutes fast for travellers' benefit. The date is 2 August 1980.

55012 *Crepello* has just brought in the empty coaching stock (ECS) for the 0950 Edinburgh–Plymouth (1V93) train.*Crepello* sits at Waverly just before working back to Haymarket MPD.The date is 2 August 1980.

55003 heading off Forth Rail Bridge with 1240 Aberdeen–Edinburgh.

55021 at Darlington heading north with the 1005 Kings Cross–Edinburgh. The date is 21 July 1980.

55018 at the same location heading south with the 1050 Edinburgh–Kings Cross on 21 July 1980.

55008 *The Green Howards* sits at York waiting to work the 1710 York-Kings Cross train on 4 October 1980. This was the only Deltic to carry the crests for its whole life. This loco was withdrawn on 31 December 1981 and cut up at Doncaster Works during August 1982.

The nameplate and crest from 55008.

55006 comes over the Border Bridge at Berwick with 0550 Kings Cross–Aberdeen train. On this day the Deltic worked right through to Aberdeen.

55012 races through Burnmouth with a train for Edinburgh.

Haymarket MPD on 13 October 1979. *Meld* sits waiting its next turn of duty.

55017 at Haymarket surrounded by other Deltics on the same day. 55008 is in the foreground and 55007 in the background.

The cab of 55017.

55021 awaits the 'off' at Doncaster on 8 January 1981, with 1005 Kings Cross-York service.

Above, below and overleaf: 55008 at the Hexthorpe bridge, Doncaster, on 21 February 1981 (0A26). This loco is reversing on to the stock for 1A26.

55004 at Joppa, near Edinburgh, with 0550 Kings Cross-Aberdeen (1S12). The date is 3 January 1981. This loco replaced 55011 at York due to engine failure.

55017 approaching Joppa with the 1425 Edinburgh–Newcastle (1E15). The Deltic is leaving a plume of smoke over Portobello in the usual Deltic style. It is the same day as the previous photograph. This is a part of Edinburgh that has changed over the years and looks very different today.

55005, after working 0550 Kings Cross–Aberdeen (1S12), passes through Princes Street Gardens heading to Haymarket MPD on 17 January 1981.

55015 in full flight approaching Craigentinny CS a couple of miles into the journey. The exhaust trail took a few minutes to disperse.

Opposite above: 55016 passing Craigentinny on 24 January 1981 with the 0950 Edinburgh-Plymouth train. This was a common Deltic turn and just after this photograph was taken the driver opened up the throttle leaving a cloud of blue/grey exhaust over Portobello.

Opposite below: 55015 prepares at Edinburgh to operate the 0950 (1V93) on 14 February 1981. This was the first time *Tulyar* had appeared with the plaque on the front of the loco. This was to commemorate the locos taking part in the Rainhill Cavalcade in May 1980. The plaque was presented by 'The Deltic Preservation Society', and prolonged the life of this Deltic with British Rail in spite of being more overdue than *Crepello* for overhaul.

55008 passing Abbeyhill, a few minutes from Waverley, with the 0550 (1S12) on a murky Saturday. The date is 7 February 1981.

Above: 55017 sits at Haymarket MPD on 4 April 1981. This loco operated a special from Edinburgh–Macclesfield (1Z09) later in the day, leaving Edinburgh at 1825.

Opposite page: 55010 approaching Carstairs Junction with 2215 Kings Cross–Aberdeen (1S70) on 5 July 1981. Sunday was a popular day for engineering works on the ECML, causing diversions for some trains. Due to the slow nature of the sleeper services they were first choice to be diverted. They made an interesting sight on the WCML. 55010 arrived at 0616 on Carstairs loop and left at 0645. Late running sleeper trains did not seem to be a high priority for British Rail at the time.

55016 approaching Rossington crossing with 1D02 Kings Cross-Hull train on 21 February 1981.

55013 passing Thorne North station, on the Hull line with the 1A18 Hull-Kings Cross train. The Hull-Kings Cross trains were quite commonly Deltic-hauled for the final years of service. The fastest locomotive-hauled train in Britain in 1979/80 was the Hull Executive.

55018 leaving Doncaster with 0933 Hull-Kings Cross (1A13) on 21 February 1981.

55021 at Hexthorpe bridge with 1L43 1403 Kings Cross-York on 21 February 1981. A common sight during these days was an enthusiast with head and camera through the window of each coach on Deltic-hauled trains.

55021 eases through Longniddry station, East Lothian, with the 0550 (1S12) on 4 April 1981. The Deltic was probably doing about 70mph but could not be heard until it had gone under the bridge at the station.

55018 in the evening sun at Meadowbank, Edinburgh, with the 1707 Edinburgh–Newcastle local stopping train. This service was not guaranteed to be hauled by a Deltic but with five on shed at Haymarket MPD that Saturday afternoon, there was a good chance one would appear in this train. The other Deltics available that afternoon were 8, 17, 21 and 22

55017 has just arrived at Edinburgh with 1S08 0705 Newcastle–Edinburgh. The driver was having problems with the steam-heating pipe from the loco, causing a leak. It created an interesting effect. After about five minutes the problem was solved. The date is 18 April 1981.

55018 on the Tay Bridge with 1S12, heading north to Aberdeen. The date is 11 April 1981. *Ballymoss* replaced *Royal Scots Grey* at Edinburgh, which had hauled the train from London.

55018 sits under the semaphore signals at Aberdeen waiting to operate the 1630 Aberdeen–Leeds on 11 April 1981.

The colour light signals can be seen but are not yet operational. Aberdeen station has been modernised and is totally different today.

55017 at Princes Street Gardens, approaching Edinburgh Waverley with the 1240 Aberdeen-Edinburgh train. The date is 20 April 1981. Enthusiasts crowd the windows of the train to witness the Deltic in action. This would be impossible today as the windows are all sealed for Health & Safety reasons.

55008 arriving at Edinburgh with 1S27, the 1930 Plymouth-Edinburgh on 18 April 1981. This Deltic operated the 0950 Edinburgh-Plymouth (1V93) earlier in the day and was taken off at York. It then worked back to Edinburgh on the northbound 1S27. This was the usual operating procedure for this train. If a Deltic was on the southbound train it was more than likely that the loco would return late afternoon – two chances to see a Deltic in operation.

55008, having been taken off the 1S27 above and being given a good wash at Haymarket MPD. If there were no problems with the locomotive on this service it would normally operate a sleeper train to London later in the day. The date is 18 April 1981.

55022 with the extra 1155 Edinburgh-Kings Cross train at Newhailes, south of Edinburgh. The date is 18 April 1981. Deltics operated a lot of relief and extra trains on holidays and the summer months.

55008 with 1V93 at Calton Tunnel Edinburgh. The date is 18 April 1981.

55008 at Portobello, Edinburgh, with 1S12. Since it was a Bank Holiday, 20 April 1981, this train started at York rather than at London Kings Cross.

55004 at Portobello with the extra 1150 Edinburgh–Kings Cross train for the Bank Holiday. The Deltic operated the ECS to Dundee where this train started, even though it was officially a Edinburgh–Kings Cross train.

55004 passing Turnhouse north of Edinburgh, heading to Aberdeen with 1S12 on 2 May 1981.

55019 leaving Edinburgh with 1V93 0950 Plymouth train on 2 May 1981. The station shunter sits in the background. It has been known on occasions that a Deltic would perform this mundane job due to breakdown of the shunter.

55019 reverses onto the stock for the above train. The Deltic in the background is 55008 waiting for the green light out of the station, to make its way to Haymarket MPD. The *Green Howards* brought in 1S08 earlier in the day. The date is 2 May 1981.

55004 passing Meadowbank, five minutes before Edinburgh, with 1S12 (0550 Edinburgh–Kings Cross). The Deltic arrived unannounced, making its way to Edinburgh with ease. It appeared to be making no effort at all.

55004 heading south of the Forth bridge on 2 May 1981 with 1E26 (1630 Aberdeen–York). It was usual operating procedure for 1S12 to Aberdeen to operate 1E26 south-bound.

55019 at Peterborough with the 0933 Hull–Kings Cross on 4 May 1981.

The same Deltic approaching Peterborough later in the day with 1L44, the 1603 Kings Cross–York. The shrinking Deltic fleet was getting well utilised.

1E35, the 2025 Edinburgh/Kings Cross, was diagrammed for Deltic haulage and 55013 did the 'honours' on the evening of Friday 15 May 1981. The loco looked in good condition but the journey proved eventful. The Deltic left Edinburgh in the usual magnificent style with great sound and exhaust trail from the mighty Napier engines. As the journey progressed it was obvious the Deltic was struggling and losing time as the train headed south. By York *The Black Watch* could go no further. The problem was caused by a burnt-out load regulator and the loco would be repaired at York MPD. Fortunately, another Deltic was spare at York and 55013 was replaced with 55008. About twenty minutes of lost time was made up and the train arrived at Kings Cross without further mishap.

55022 arrives at Kings Cross in the early hours of Saturday morning (at 0617), 16 May 1981, with the 2315 Edinburgh-Kings Cross sleeper train (1E42). 55022 was only about seventeen minutes behind the 2250 Edinburgh-Kings Cross, which 55016 had brought in. A quiet Kings Cross was beginning to vibrate with the wonderful music of the Deltics.

55016 at the head of ECS and 55018 at the head of 0805 Kings Cross-Hull. Due to technical difficulties, *Ballymoss* left Kings Cross fifteen minutes late. In these days Kings Cross was a lively place with the sight and the sound of the Deltics. The large domes of the station sent the soundwaves of Deltics and other diesels round with a gentle hint of exhaust fumes, contrasting with today's electric traction creating a sterile environment. The date was 16 May 1981 and it was a busy day for Deltics at the Cross, working several trains and various ECS workings in between.

Ballymoss later the same day at Kings Cross, when she returned with a train from Hull.

55007 arriving at Kings Cross with 1A13 0933 Hull-Kings Cross on 16 May 1981. The platforms at all ECML stations were busy with rail enthusiasts watching the final movements of the Deltics. Today's platforms are less busy.

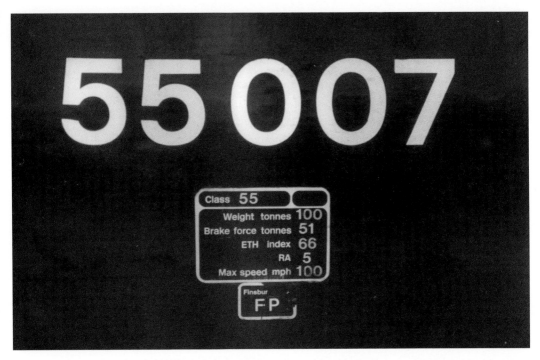

Class 55		
Weight tonnes	100	
Brake force tonnes	51	
ETH index	66	
RA	5	
Max speed mph	100	
Finsbur FP		

Above and below: 55007 approaching the 'blocks', as it was called, at Kings Cross with 1A13, 16 May 1981.

55007 takes a breather at 'The Cross'. The Deltics always attracted more interest than other locomotives. (See previous photo of 7 arriving at Kings Cross on p.41)

Pinza is released of its coaches and is heading to Finsbury Park MPD for refuelling (see previous photo. graph). The loco is named after a racehorse that won the Derby and King George VI and Queen Elizabeth Stakes in 1953. The Deltic was named at Doncaster on 22 June 1961.

55016 is getting a routine check at at Finsbury Park MPD on 16 May 1981.

55016 is then put outside awaiting its next turn of duty. The other Deltic is 55008. *The Green Howards* worked 1L43, the 1405 Kings Cross-York, and 55016 operated 1L42, the 1220 Kings Cross-York. The date is 16 May 1981.

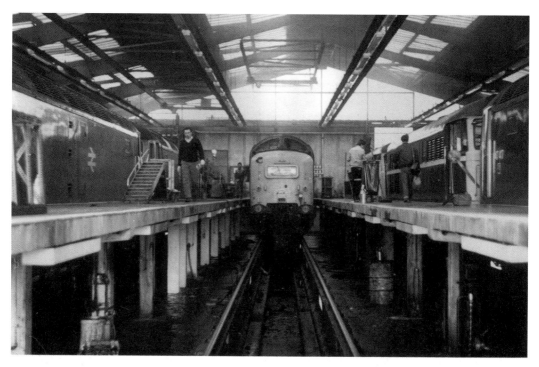

55022 at Finsbury Park on 16 May 1981. This Deltic was getting ready to operate 1D02, the 1205 Kings Cross–Hull train. This loco was named at Edinburgh on 18 February 1962.

55022 powering through Finsbury Park station with 1D02, the 1205 Kings Cross–Hull on the same day as the previous photograph. The rain is pouring down making a it a right dull day in north London.

Fifteen minutes later, 55016 is at the same location with 1L42, the 1220 Kings Cross–York. This was the busiest section of the ECML. With express, semi-fast, commuter and goods trains using this section, any breakdowns caused major problems at times. Thankfully, this did not happen too often.

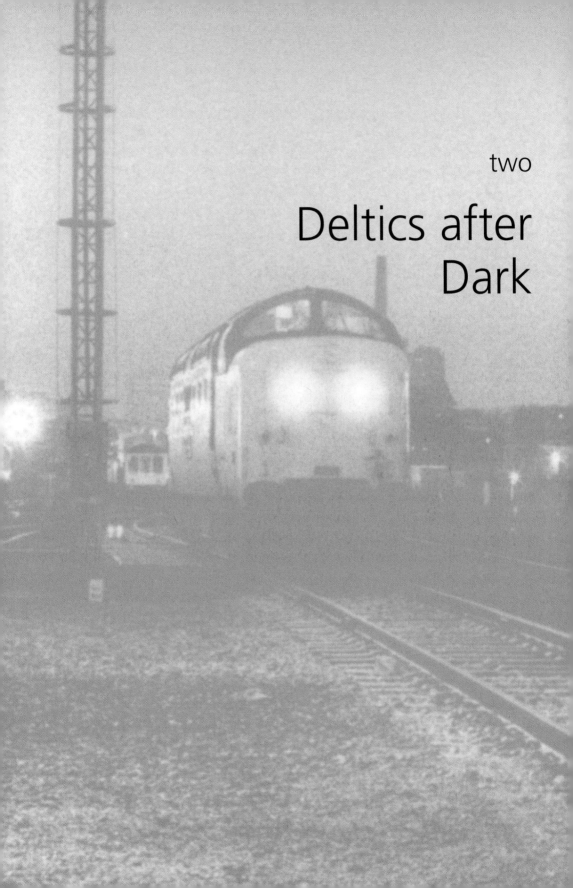

two

Deltics after
Dark

The Deltics after dark were an interesting sight. The various light effects made interesting and different photographs. Here, 55021 has just returned to Edinburgh Haymarket MPD at 1615 on 21 November 1981. This loco worked the 1215 Edinburgh-Kings Cross as far as Newcastle in place of an HST that had failed. The Deltic had worked into Edinburgh on 1S08, the 0705 Newcastle-Edinburgh, in the early morning. The castle can be seen behind the Deltic. The dark skyline gives an 'eerie' feel to this photograph.

55012 sits at Edinburgh waiting to leave with the 2315 Edinburgh-Kings Cross (1E42). The sleeper trains were quite often Deltic-hauled and with quiet platforms the 'ghost figures' did not often appear in the photographs. The date here is 23 December 1980.

55006 sits at the head of the 2250 Edinburgh–Kings Cross sleeper train on Tuesday, 23 December 1980. Earlier that night, 55006 brought into Edinburgh the stock that would form the 2230 Edinburgh–Kings Cross. It turned out to be the last appearance in Scotland for 55003 *Meld*. At 2250, 55006 left on time.

55017 sits at Edinburgh ready to work the 2225 Edinburgh–Kings Cross train. It was a very murky night with temperatures well below zero. The date is 27 December 1980.

55004 preparing to haul the 2230 Edinburgh-Kings Cross on Friday 19 December 1980. The driver is revving one engine to test the dials in the cab. This created a great sound in the station and exhaust fumes that could intoxicate an enthusiast. Today's electric traction does not have this wonderful effect.

55022 sits at the head of the 2025 Edinburgh-Kings Cross on a wet Edinburgh Friday evening on 12 December 1980. Any time I travelled on this train it was busy, with Deltic enthusiasts mainly, I must add.

55010 sits at the head of the 2210 Edinburgh-Kings Cross on Saturday 7 March 1981. Vandals tried to remove one of the locomotive's nameplates so British Rail wisely removed the plate for safe-keeping. The locomotive was named at Dumfries on 8 May 1965. As a consequence of the attempted theft 55010 operated her final couple of years with only one plate.

The remaining plate.

Above: 55022 rests at Kings Cross after the journey in the early hours of Saturday morning. The mail bags are being off-loaded at an as yet still quiet Kings Cross.

Below: 55018 at Kings Cross before working the 0550 Kings Cross–Aberdeen (1S12), on 13 December 1980.

Above and below: Ballymoss was a popular member of the class, named after the racehorse that won the St Leger, King George VI and Queen Elizabeth Stakes in 1958. The loco was named at Doncaster on 24 November 1961.

55014 at Newcastle with the 1E43 sleeper service. The train left Edinburgh for Newcastle but went via Carlisle because of engineering work on the ECML. The train had a stop-over at Newcastle before heading south. The date is 29 August 1981.

55021 at 'the blocks' with a train from York. The time is 2130, when the station was going through a quiet spell before sleeper trains were readed for service. The date is 25 October 1980.

55016 at Edinburgh on a wet evening with the 2025 Edinburgh-Kings Cross on Friday 19 December 1980.

55011 sits in a shower of rain at Edinburgh on 12 December 1980, waiting to work the 1945 Edinburgh–Leeds. This train started at Aberdeen and in my experience was hauled by a class 47 to Edinburgh then changed for a Deltic, or occassionally another class 47.

55017 had a busy Christmas Eve in 1981. It worked the 0550 Kings Cross–Aberdeen right through, then 1630 Aberdeen-York uninterupted. It is seen here at Edinburgh awaiting departure for York.

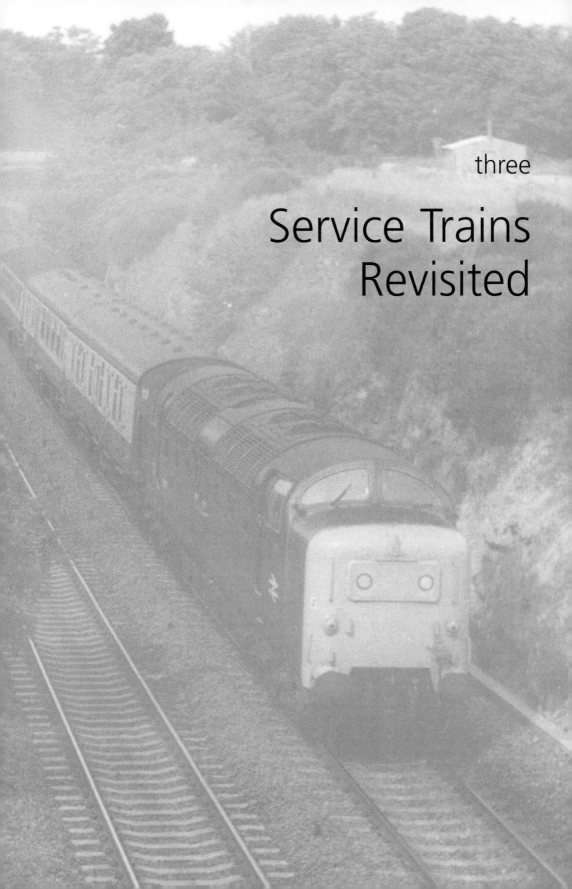

three

Service Trains
Revisited

Monday 25 May 1981 was an easy day for 55002. The locomotive looked superb in two-tone green with original British Railways emblem. The York City coat-of-arms can be seen above the number. The Deltic is seen here at Portobello, Edinburgh, heading south with the 1707 Edinburgh-Newcastle. This train sometimes had as many as twelve Mk1 coaches, which No.2 handled easily, accelerating leaving a cloud over the surrounding area which lasted five minutes after the train passed. The Deltic had sat quietly at Haymarket all day after bringing in the 0705 Newcastle-Edinburgh.

55013 takes ECS from Edinburgh Craigentinny CS on 25 May 1981. *The Black Watch* was named at Dundee on 16 January 1963. This Deltic worked an unusual train on 16 December 1981, the 0723 Peterborough-Kings Cross. The locomotive failed at Wood Green and had to be helped into London by a class 31. This turned out to 13's last train. The Deltic was withdrawn four days later.

Royal Scots Grey arriving at Edinburgh with 1S27 0730 Plymouth-Edinburgh on 30 May 1981. This loco worked 0950 Edinburgh-Plymouth as far as York, then 1S27 as diagrammed to Edinburgh.

55002 passing Craigentinny CS with 1S08 Newcastle-Edinburgh on 13 June 1981.

55016 at Newhailes, Edinburgh on 8 July 1981, with the same service train, 1S08. This train left Kings Cross travelling to Newcastle where it had a stop-over, continuing on to Edinburgh as the 0705 1S08. This train, in my experience, was a regular Deltic turn up until October/November 1981.

55010 at Carstairs Junction on 5 July 1981 with the sleeper train from London (1S70, 2215 Kings Cross–Aberdeen). Parts of the psychiatric penal institution can be seen in the background. This was a serene time of the morning with only the gentle hum of the powerful Napier engines to be heard over the fields.

55015 at Carstairs Junction on the same day, just over an hour later, with 1S72, 2230 Kings Cross–Edinburgh sleeper.

Goswick signal box, Northumberland, on the ECML. The main-line used to have many small signal boxes controlling level crossings and signals. Today most are gone, replaced by large, modern, electronic complexes controlling tracks many miles from their location.

Goswick signal box.

55004 passing the signal box with 1S85, 1030 Kings Cross-Edinburgh on Wednesday 8 July 1981. The summer season schedules created some 'interesting' relief trains. If a Deltic was available there was a good chance they would operate these trains.

55004 approaching Dunbar with the 0550 Kings Cross-Aberdeen on 25 July 1981. 55004 was taken off the train at Edinburgh.

55004 is reversing onto the stock for the 1455 Edinburgh-Aberdeen on 25 July 1981. This was a bonus train as it was rarely worked by a Deltic.

55004 at Aberdeen preparing to work the 1830 Aberdeen–Edinburgh on 25 July 1981. It was a busy day for 55004.

55019 leaving Edinburgh in style with the 0950 Edinburgh–Plymouth cross-country on Tuesday 25 August 1981.

55007 at Wallyford, East Lothian, with the 0950 Edinburgh-Plymouth (1S27) on 11 July 1981. By this time the 'Racehorses' had lost their white cabs that had been applied by Finsbury Park MPD. This was because they were transferred to York MPD for the final months of service.

55007 returning to Edinburgh on the same day with 1S27, 0730 Plymouth-Edinburgh.

55008 during the early summer sunshine with 1S08 0705 Newcastle–Edinburgh on 29 July 1981. The location is Newhailes, Lothian.

55015 at Portobello, heading south with a heavy loaded 1E29, 1718 Edinburgh-Newcastle train, on the final day of July 1981.

55017 at Penmanshiel cutting in the evening sunshine with 1E29, 1718 Edinburgh–Newcastle on 29 July 1981. The tunnel at Penmanshiel had to be abandoned due to a serious accident. A team of engineers were in the tunnel doing repair work when the tunnel wall collapsed, killing one and injuring several railmen. British Rail could not retrieve the man's body due to the dangerous state of the tunnel, adding more misery to the man's family– a very sad day in rail history.

A generator plate from 55017.

55017 at East Barns, south of Dunbar, with 1S12, the 0550 Kings Cross-Aberdeen, on 29 July 1981.

55002 at Burnmouth heading north with 1S76 on 29 July 1981. The train is running twenty minutes late. This is one of the most picturesque areas of the whole ECML, with the good weather helping to create a nice scene.

55004 leaving Newcastle with ECS from the 1718 Edinburgh-Newcastle train which it had worked into the city. The date is 1 August 1981.

55004 approaching Markie crossing just north of East Linton, East Lothian, with 1V93 on 15 August 1981. These crossings must be even more dangerous today with electric traction, and no warning of an approaching train.

55018 has just arrived at York with 1205 Kings Cross-York on 3 August 1981.

55010 weaves into York on 3 August 1981, with the 1403 Kings Cross-York train. Today's scene is very different, a much simplified track layout and electric wires obliterating the view.

Two photographs at Penmanshiel cutting on Saturday 29 August 1981. This is 55022 with 1V93 heading south. It was a misty day.

55017 heading south with 1E1O. One of Deltic 17's nose-ends was unique in that it did not have a step at the bottom like all the rest of the Deltics. This was because a new end was fabricated at Doncaster during repair.

Approaching Dunbar with 1S12 on 15 August 1981. This train stopped at Dunbar and was slowing down to cross onto the single line into the station. A Deltic on a non-stop train could be heard for a while before it could be seen as wind carried the sound of the locomotive powering up the steep gradient.

55017 at East Barns, south of Dunbar, with 1E1O. This was a summer-only working from Dundee-Kings Cross. The date is 15 August 1981.

55004 racing through Dunbar with a special train for the Edinburgh Festival, on 25 August 1981. The train was from the North East of England. The Deltic was working on one engine only.

55017 was only four minutes behind with 1S12, which was stopping at Dunbar.

55021 powering up the gradient towards Dunbar with 1S76, on 25 August 1981. This train was a summer-only working.

Overleaf: 55017 at the Penmanshiel cutting on 19 September 1981 with 1S27, the 0730 Plymouth–Edinburgh. The driver has just turned the power off, leaving a blue-grey plume of exhaust smoke which took a few minutes to dissipate.

55017 near Stenton crossing, East Lothian, with 1V93 on 19 September 1981. This was a heavy train with twelve coaches, which 17 worked with ease. This crossing had a pedestrian footbridge which gave a good vantage point of the main line.

55009 heading north at Burnmouth with 1S12 on 19 September 1981. This view today is obliterated by masts and wires for electric traction. No gentle hum of the Napier engines, just silent death with no advanced warning of arrival.

55013 decelerates for a stop at Dunbar with 1S12 on 12 September 1981.

55017 takes a rest at Haymarket MPD on 19 September 1981. *The Durham Light Infantry* had worked 1S27 into Edinburgh earlier (see photograph taken at Penmanshiel).

55008 at East Linton, East Lothian, with 1E29, the 1718 Edinburgh-Newcastle, on 12 September 1981. The train is running ten minutes late. The evening sun on the side of the locomotive gives a nice moody effect to this photograph.

55013 sweeps through Portobello, Edinburgh, with the 0730 Plymouth-Edinburgh train on 25 September 1981, running thirty-three minutes late. The track coming in from the right was the old Waverley route from Carlisle and the Borders. Since this route closed nearly thirty years ago, there has been talk ef opening the line up again, but with no avail to date.

55019 arriving at Haymarket MPD on Friday 25 September 1981. This Deltic had just worked the 0550 Kings Cross–Aberdeen as far as Edinburgh. In the background 55016 can be seen, this locomotive having worked 1S08 earlier in the day.

55002 at Haymarket on 25 September 1981. This Deltic was used for ECS earlier in the day at Craigentinny and, during the day it did various shunting duties. It left Edinburgh later in day with 1E29, the 1718 Edinburgh–Newcastle train.

Haymarket MPD, 25 September 1981. 55016 is waiting patiently for its next turn of duty. Not long after this photograph was taken, the Deltic left the depot heading for Waverley station ready to work the 1455 Edinburgh–Aberdeen train.

55009 sits at York MPD on Saturday 10 October 1981. This was one of the four Deltics that was to be prepared to operate a series of Deltic railtours. 55009 was to be totally repainted and work started the following day. *Alycidon* appeared the following weekend in superb condition.

Deltic 9 at York MPD (see previous photograph).

55008 sits at York MPD on 10 October 1981. One engine of the Deltic failed two days previous and the locomotive was sent light engine to York. 55008 was restricted to one engine until 1 November 1981 when it got a unit from 55004 which had been withdrawn.

55010 at Haymarket MPD on 8 November 1981. This was a sad day as 55011 was withdrawn, leaving only thirteen locomotives.

Opposite above: 55011 sits in sidings at York MPD on 10 October 1981. This Deltic was also restricted to one engine only and ran in this condition until withdrawal on 8 November 1981.

Opposite below: 55008 and 55017 sit at York on 10 October 1981.

A close-up view of 55010 and class 47 (as on p.87).

four

By the
Seaside

The two most unusual destinations for the Deltics in the final year were Whitby and Oban. Both seaside towns had two visits, 55002 going to Whitby and 55021 going to Oban.

55002 approaches Newcastle with ECS for the special to Whitby on Sunday 30 August 1981.

55002 leaving Newcastle with the special on 30 August 1981.

The train went through Sunderland, Hartlepool and on to Battersby, where the locomotive had to run round the stock to continue on to Middlesborough, then Whitby. It is here seen at Battersby with the crowds spilling out on to the platform on 30 August 1981.

55002 is seen here approaching Whitby on 2 August 1981, with the first special to the town.

The quiet of Whitby is shattered by the arrival of the special on 2 August 1981.

Whitby is a popular holiday destination, particularly with the older generation. The special left Newcastle at 0932 and arrived at Whitby at 1210. This is the 2 August 1981 outing.

55002 waits to take the return trip to Newcastle on 2 August 1981. The train left Whitby at 1727, arriving back at Newcastle at 2000 on the dot.

55002 passes a preserved class 35 Hymek diesel at Grosmont on 2 August 1981. The North Yorks Moor Railway is the home of The Deltic Preservation Society Deltics.

Oban was the destination for two unusual Deltic railtours in the month of August 1981. Oban is a fishing town on the West Highlands of Scotland. It is also a big tourist destination. A Deltic was selected because the Scottish class 37s did not have electric train heating at the time and class 47s had too high an axle load for the West Highland line. An appropriate choice of Deltic was 55021 *Argyll & Sutherland Highlander*. This loco operated both specials on 2 August and the 23rd of the month. I have featured the second tour on 23 August 1981.

Haymarket MPD turned out the Deltic in superb condition.

On the way to Oban, passing Summerston, North Glasgow. The nice weather, an Indian summer, made this a great day.

Above and below: McCaig's folly can be seen in the background, a landmark of Oban which makes the town instantly recognisable. The headboard used was a modified Silver Jubilee of 1977. The English flag was replaced with the lion rampant, and the title 'West Highlands Tour' added.

Above and below: The Deltic runs round the train at Oban. 55021 was at the time allocated to York MPD, but Haymarket MPD turned the locomotive out in great condition complete with a shed badge from Haymarket.

55021 reverses the train into the platform for the return journey.

The Deltic is ready for the return journey. Two class 37s sit at other platforms with a goods train and a passenger train for Glasgow. At this time, Oban station had several platforms and a large glass canopy over the entrance. Today this has gone, replaced by a shopping centre. All that remains are the two platforms on the left.

The return journey begins at Oban. The signalman waits in front of the box with the single-line token for the driver's assistant.

The gradient out of Oban is quite steep. The Deltic managed it with ease, creating a magnificent sight for all assembled photographers.

The scenery in the West Highlands is superb, with the Deltic adding to the view.

The run between Oban and Glasgow was easy for the mighty Napier engines of the Deltic, causing a build-up of lubricant oil on the collector drums of the power units. At Eastfield MPD, where the line joins the main Glasgow-Edinburgh line, the driver applied more power, causing an excessive exhaust plume. Not healthy, but quite a photogenic sight. This great day was nearing to an end. All that remained was a run through to Edinburgh, via Falkirk Grahamston. Most of this section was at high speed giving the engines a good 'work out' and a great end to a truly remarkable day.

five

Railtours

There were a great number of railtours with Deltic haulage right from the early years of the class. The greatest number were in the final year of operation. Four Deltics were chosen for the special workings, these being 55002, 55009, 55015 and 55022. These locomotives had to be in good condition and York MPD serviced and, in some cases, repainted the Deltics. In this chapter I have covered some of the railtours that were witnessed by myself.

55002 on the WCML at Symington with The Deltic Preservation Society special, the North Briton. The train was fifty minutes late due to bad weather. This was one of the first that year, the date being Saturday 25 April 1981.

55002 leaves Dunbar with the DPS North Briton on 25 April 1981. This 'special' went from Edinburgh to York on the ECML, then, after arriving via Carlisle, to Edinburgh on the WCML. The headboard was allowed back on the Deltic due to the fact there were no electric wires on this section of the ECML at that time.

55002 made history on Monday, 4 May 1981, by becoming the first Deltic on to a privately owned railway line. It happened on the Nene Valley Railway (NVR), Peterborough. Here, the special is seen at March, with the 'Deltic Fenman'.

Left: Here, the special is seen entering Wansford (NVR).

Below: The special at Peterborough. The driver's assistant hands back the single-line token.

55002 runs round the stock at Peterborough.

55009 worked a special on 17 October 1981. The Deltic was just out of York MPD after a repaint and is in beautiful condition in this photograph, here seen at Burntisland. The Deltic worked from Newcastle to Perth, then 'light diesel' to Aberdeen, then worked the special to Newcastle.

Above: The special at Burntisland, 17 October 1981.

Left: 55009 is taken off at Perth

55002 operates The Celtic Deltic on Saturday 31 October 1981 at Dunbar, East Lothian. This railtour ran from Kings Cross to Edinburgh then back to Peterborough (1F52).

At Edinburgh, preparing to head south with The Celtic Deltic, 55002 is in good condition. This railtour was organised by British Rail and was a particulary popular event, Peterborough being at the heart of 'Deltic country'!

55009 at Carlisle on 14 November 1981 with the Deltic Cumbrian. This special went from Kings Cross-Leeds-Carlisle-Newcastle-Kings Cross.

Passing Kingmoor shed, Carlisle, with 55009 in charge.

55002 at Craiglockhart Junction, Edinburgh on 21 November 1981, with the Deltic Scotsman. This special was from York–Inverkeithing via the Settle & Carlisle line and Newcastle. At the time, this railway round Edinburgh was used for goods trains only and a passenger train here was unusual. The train was, however, over an hour late due to wheelslip at Carlisle. On the southbound trip from Edinburgh to York, 55013 took charge because 55002 needed fuel and water at Haymarket.

55009 on the WCML, slowing down for Carstairs on 28 November 1981, with a railtour from Newcastle-Carlisle-Edinburgh-Newcastle.

55009 heading to Aberdeen from Edinburgh with the Grampian Deltic. Heavy snow was encountered on the way. The date was Saturday 12 December 1981. This special went from Edinburgh to Aberdeen via Perth.

At Aberdeen for re-fuelling.

six

The Last Deltics

FAREWELL
TO THY
GREATNESS

1F 50   21 82

This chapter, by definition, is the saddest of the whole book. I have included last appearances, workings, railtours, etc.

55003 sits at the head of the 2230 Edinburgh-Kings Cross train on Tuesday 23 December 1980 at Waverley. This was last *Meld's* appearance in Scotland. 55003 worked a Kings Cross-Scotland train five days later, but failed at Newcastle. The locomotive was taken to Gateshead MPD and never crossed the border again.

Above and below: 55003 makes a sad site at Doncaster Works scrap sidings on 21 February 1981.

Above and below: 55005 sits outside Doncaster Works two weeks after withdrawal from service. The nameplates have been removed for 'safe-keeping'.

Above: 55012 sits at Finsbury Park MPD on 16 May 1981. The locomotive was taken out of traffic two days before for a C examination, but a decision was taken to withdraw the Deltic on 18 May 1981. The locomotive was due for a major overhaul at Doncaster, but this would not be cost-effective.

55015 with the Hadrian Flyer on 5 December 1981. The train has just left Appleby, on the Settle & Carlisle line, the last time a Deltic was used this route.

55015 at Appleby.

55015 takes the train through the wash at Kingmoor depot, Carlisle. The railtour went from Peterborough to Carlisle and Newcastle.

55008 sits at Edinburgh after working the 1830 Glasgow–Edinburgh service. The train was about thirty minutes late. This was the last Deltic to visit Glasgow, on 24 December 1981.

55019 sits at the head of the 1945 Edinburgh–York train at Waverley on 31 December 1981. The train originated at Aberdeen as the 1630 to York (1E26). *Royal Highland Fusilier* was put on the train at Edinburgh. This was the last service train hauled by a Deltic on British Rail. A headboard and wreath was placed on the locomotive at Darlington for the final run into York.

A Deltic Preservation Society (D.P.S.) stand at N.R.M.

55015 *Tulyar* arrives in Edinburgh with the northbound leg of the Deltic Scotsman Farewell to a large crowd of wellwishers. The weather was appropriate rain. *Tulyar* was a few minutes late and had a wreath on the front of her cab.

Opposite page: 55022 *Royal Scots Grey* sits at Haymarket for the last time on Saturday 2 January 1982. The Deltic is ready to work the last railtour from Edinburgh–Kings Cross, the Deltic Scotsman Farewell. An appropriate headboard is on the locomotive.

55022 reverses onto the stock for the southbound leg of the Deltic Scotsman Farewell. This was the last Deltic out of Edinburgh, bringing to an end an era of twenty years' service. It was a sad day for the thousands that witnessed the departure of a truly great locomotive.

A sad view at Doncaster Works scrap sidings on Friday, 29 January 1982. A line of Deltic awaits the cutter's torch. They are, from front to back: 55007, 55021, 55010, 55019, 55004, 55022, 55009, 55016, 55005, 55013, 55008 and 55017. At the end of February 1982, there was an open day at Doncaster Works to show the Deltics that remained.

The same line-up taken from the large crane.

Opposite: 55019, saved and working on the North Yorkshire Moors Railway (NYMR).

seven

The Afterlife

A few Deltics have been preserved for future generations to enjoy. It was a truly remarkable locomotive class and its like will never be seen again. In a rather ironic twist to the tale of the Deltics, some have returned to main-line service and have been leased out for use on passenger trains again.

55019 on the NYMR.

A replica nameplate and crest.

55009, saved on the NYMR.

55009 on the NYMR.

Other titles published by Tempus

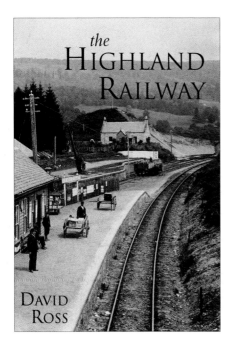

The Highland Railway

DAVID ROSS

Good news from the Scottish Highlands was a rarity in the mid-nineteenth century. But, from 1855, a railway system began to spread there, planned, financed, and managed entirely within the region. The Highland Railway, eventually extending from Perth to Wick, and from Keith to Kyle of Lochalsh, became the biggest industrial concern and employer in the Highlands, and one of the most individual of British railway companies. This book records its fascinating history.

978 0 7524 3479 1

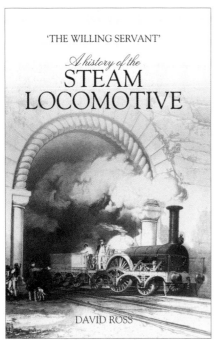

The Willing Servant A History of the Steam Locomotive

DAVID ROSS

After a slow beginning, the railway locomotive spread across the face of the earth. It was the sustaining force of industrial growth in Britain and Europe. It helped to bolster the Russian Revolution, and it opened up vast colonial territories. In peace and war, it became humanity's most willing servant. This book traces not only the history of design, construction and use, but the intriguing story of human involvement.

978 0 7524 2986 1

If you are interested in purchasing other books published by Tempus, or in case you have difficulty finding any Tempus books in your local bookshop, you can also place orders directly through our website

www.tempus-publishing.com